THE SOCIAL STRUGGLE

Published by Floodlit Dreams Ltd, 2019.

A CIP catalogue record for this book is available from the British Library.

ISBN 978-0992658571

Floodlit Dreams Ltd
5-6 George St
St Albans
Herts
AL3 4ER

www.floodlitdreams.com

Cover and inside design by Steve Leard
Words by Woody and Kleiny with Seth Burkett

THE SOCIAL STRUGGLE

How we took over the Internet

@WOODYANDKLEINY

CONTENTS

CHAPTER 1
FIRED

CHAPTER 1

FIRED 🔥

Woody: Is this thing recording?

Kleiny: Don't say that, mate, you'll scare us.

Woody: Don't worry, I was just having a laugh. Everything we say is being recorded, honest.

Kleiny: Nice one. Shall we write this book then?

Woody: Yeah, go on then. Where shall we start?

Kleiny: How about the beginning, when we first created our YouTube channel?

Woody: When was that? Six years ago?

Kleiny: 2013.

Woody: That was actually one of our low points. It was cool to start our

On set doing what we do best.

own YouTube channel, but we only did it because we'd just lost our jobs as presenters. We were fronting a show called 433 on the /football YouTube channel when, after six months, /football decided to cancel our show.

Kleiny: Before that we were football freestylers. We'd been on Britain's Got Talent in 2009 and were the first double act to perform synchronised freestyle football on stage. If you want to gain recognition as entertainers then what better platform than Britain's Got Talent?

Woody: There were quite a few freestylers auditioning, but they were all auditioning as individuals. We've always wanted to set ourselves apart. Because we were unique, we were put straight in front of the judges. We went on stage and Piers Morgan asked us if we thought we could win the competition.

'Well, Piers,' I replied, 'we wouldn't be here if we didn't believe we could do something. We wouldn't want to waste our time, your time and all these people in the crowd's time if we didn't believe we could win it, so we're going to go and win it.'

That got one hell of a cheer.

I don't usually get nerves on stage, but during that performance I was

so nervous for Kleiny. I've always felt like an older brother to him. There was no need to be nervous. Kleiny smashed it. His timing, transitions, executions were all flawless. He smashed it. We smashed it.

Kleiny: I can't really remember it to be honest.

Woody: All four of the judges put us through. They all said 'yes' to us. Simon Cowell called us 'the Ant and Dec' of freestyle. But when it came to deciding the acts for the semi-final, we were told we weren't going to be put through. There had been a freestyler on the previous year's competition and he'd had a bit of a nightmare on stage. The producers wanted to move away from all things football, but had been so impressed by us that they held onto us as a reserve act.

That was it. We never heard back from the show. But the experience had propelled us into the public consciousness. It had proved we could entertain at a high level. Someone even bought woodyandkleiny. com and tried to sell it to us for £15,000! No thanks. We had to take woodyandkleinyfreestyle.com.

Kleiny: After Britain's Got Talent I joined Woody in becoming a UEFA skills expert, working with elite footballers and presenting videos tutorials on how to do specific skills. We were becoming more prominent and gaining traction within the industry. But just when things were going well, I got a serious back injury and had to cut back on football and freestyling.

Woody: Fortunately, the presenting opportunity came up not long after. It was nuts. /football were looking for two presenters to host a chat show and they got loads of people in for a screentest. We were invited to audition because the programme was

going to be about football and they wanted two people who could hold a good conversation, look half-decent on screen and had a few football skills. Essentially, the people they chose had to have a good knowledge of football and a personality to match. We got to the audition room and found ourselves amongst all kinds of presenters. There were people who had worked on all kinds of big British TV shows.

When our turn to audition came, we were guided into a room and put in front of a camera. It was up to us to show the programme's producers what we were all about. We answered a few questions and went through a few scenarios, then after around eight minutes the lead producer, Owen, marched into the room and said: 'Stop! I've seen enough.' I looked at Kleiny and Kleiny looked at me. We both thought the same

thing: 'We've blown it. That's a wrap.' Then Owen started speaking. 'We've had this, that and the other in today,' he began, reeling off a long list of names. 'And I want you two.'

Woah. Amazing!

Kleiny: We thought we'd messed up, but Owen gave us the contracts there and then. Ten minutes after our audition we were officially presenters.

Woody: As part of the contract, we had to film two shows a week – both of them on a Sunday. One of the shows was live, while the other was a pre-record that would go out every Friday.

We loved our show. It was like the Wayne's World of Soccer AM. A bit rough and ready round the edges but a perfectly good formula. Ever since

Kleiny did his back in, we'd wanted to be TV presenters, so in a way we were living our dream.

Kleiny: Then it got cancelled.

Woody: Our shows were doing well. They were getting around 100,000 views on YouTube. Unfortunately, that wasn't enough for /football. We filmed our last show on a Sunday. Within an hour of the cameras cutting we received a call saying that we were getting fired. They wanted to go in a different direction. The show was no more.

I was absolutely deflated. So, so gutted.

To have something taken away from you that you love, through no fault of your own, is heart-breaking. Every time we filmed was fun, a real buzz. It felt like everything had been going really well.

And now we had been forced to take a step back. Again. Just when things had been going so well for us. Where were we going to go from here? Two days later, I got a phone call from Kleiny that changed everything.

Kleiny: The whole time we were presenting we had no presence on social media. Facebook existed but it wasn't nearly as big as it is now for creators. YouTube was also around, and people were just starting to have success on the platform. It got me thinking: 'Okay, one dream has ended, so what's going to come next?' I was convinced I'd found the answer.

At the time, Woody lived two minutes away from me, on the other side of a roundabout in Welwyn Garden City, Hertfordshire. I knew he needed picking up, so I told him to get himself round mine. I already had everything set up.

Woody: There was a camera waiting for me. 'Come on, Woody,' Kleiny told me. 'We're setting up a YouTube channel. Let's forget our show getting cancelled; now we go again.' Okay, I told him, let's see where this goes. Christmas was a few weeks away and Kleiny finished by telling me he'd got me a present. It was a tin can. When I opened the can a fake snake jumped out at me. It was proper old-school but still shook me up a bit. The camera recorded everything and suddenly we had our first video.

'NOW WE GO AGAIN'

CHAPTER 2
OUT OF FOCUS

CHAPTER 2

OUT OF FOCUS

Kleiny: There's an Ed Sheeran documentary called Songwriter, where Ed uses an analogy of a dirty tap to describe his early years of creating music. You go into an old house and find that it's completely run-down. You walk over to the sink, turn on the tap, and the water comes out as a dark brown liquid. You leave the tap running, and after a few minutes you get a bit of clear water. Only a bit, though, because the water soon turns brown again. Yet the longer you leave the tap on, the more regularly the clear water comes. Soon there's more clear water than brown water.

Woody: We relate to that story so much. The dark brown water represents those first ideas. At the time they seem amazing, but in reality they're not. Ed Sheeran's first songs weren't great, but he kept the tap running. He wasn't put off by the gunk. He kept creating, and every now and then clear water came: his

Kleiny: Even with Darryl's limited filming ability, we came up with some good pieces of content. We were the first people to ever do public nutmegs. We'd dribble round Leicester Square and knock the ball through the legs of random passers-by.

Then there was 'Public Referee'. We had Woody in his full Arsenal kit, Harry in a portable goal, Darryl filming, and me dressed up as a referee. That was done in Chinatown. I'd run up to random people and show them a yellow card.

'I let the first one go,' I'd yell at them, 'but that one was naughty.'

I'd then make them stand in a wall, mark a line with foam spray and shout 'No encroachment!' if they tried to walk off. 'I won't have you edging!' A lot of them walked away, but some played along. It was then down to Woody to take the free-kick.

We just had one problem: Harry is super-competitive. He wouldn't let any of the goals go in!

Darryl: I was saying to Harry: 'You have to let a goal go in. It's going to be a rubbish video if we can't even score a goal.' And what did he say? 'No way. I'm not letting one in. Nobody is going to score while I'm in goal.'

Just another photo of Darryl not looking through the lens again.

Woody: We invested a lot of money into some of those early videos. We both had football-coaching businesses, so all of the money we made from that we ploughed into our YouTube channel. There was 'Giant Beer Pong', where we bought these massive trash cans, painted them red and then bought a drone so we could film the action from above. We put a football spin on it, so rather than throw a ping-pong ball into a cup, we had to shoot a football into our opponent's bin.

We bought a massive water slide to film 'Brutal Slide Tackles'.

Darryl: Yeah, I got to take part in that one. Cheers, guys!

Kleiny: Darryl had to dribble a ball down the waterslide and then Woody would charge in from behind and slide-tackle him down the water slide. Neither of us fancied being tackled, so Darryl was the obvious option.

Woody: We hustled our way into a trampoline park to film 'Megajump Football'. That was all clear water, but obviously there was still a lot of dirty water coming out of our tap. 'Rate Your Partner' was a bad idea. That was in Leicester Square, and we asked members of the public to rate their other half out of ten. It didn't really fit in with everything else we were doing. Neither did 'Big Brother Live'. That involved approaching members of the public and convincing them that they were going to be filmed for the reality TV show Big Brother. We had an iPad that counted down from ten, then when it hit zero we told them they were live on air.

'Okay, you're going to the diary room,' we'd tell them. 'Katie Price has asked what's your favourite food and what do you make of Callum Best doing what he did at that moment? It was disgusting, wasn't it?'

Of course, Callum Best had done no such thing. We'd made the whole scenario up, but the people we interviewed played along because they didn't want to seem stupid. It was all about making fools out of them. Sometimes we'd have to push them a bit further to get an answer.

'What do you think about him touching her? It's just inappropriate, isn't it?'

It was a solid formula, and we put a spin on it to do versions with Match of the Day and other TV programmes, but what we didn't realise was that we were limiting ourselves. Big Brother wasnt globally recognised, and nobody knew the people we were talking about.

Kleiny: All of that time spent filming. All of that money invested into props. We were so convinced that at least one of those videos would go viral. But they never did. They only ever got hundreds of views. We weren't even close to making any money from our channel.

Collaboration was key to growing. We had to work with well-known YouTubers to help boost our following. But hardly any YouTubers wanted to work with us because we didn't have a following of our own, so there wasn't anything in it for them. The only option was to keep on creating content and hope that one of our videos would blow up and we'd get loads of followers.

112 views.

379 views.

It was devastating, but we had to get rid of any negative energy immediately. We couldn't let thoughts about whether the whole YouTube project was worth it affect us on our journey.

Woody: We had to keep going until we won. We couldn't lose. We don't have time to lose. How can you invest so much time and money in something and not see it through to the end? If you waste time then you have lost. And that's not what we're about. It's never been what we're about. You know why? Because all we do is win, win, win. No matter what.

CHAPTER 3
FROM SILVER SPOON TO WOODEN SPOON

CHAPTER 3

FROM SILVER SPOON TO WOODEN SPOON

Kleiny: Growing up, I used to be the most negative person in the world. Which must have appeared strange from the outside looking in, because I had pretty much everything I ever wanted.

I was born with a silver spoon in my mouth. Not literally, of course, but thanks to my family I had a very comfortable upbringing. My dad was a cameraman and my mum had her own taxi business in Barnet, so money was never an issue. We lived in a series of nice, four-bedroom houses in Barnet, Cheshunt and Potters Bar, each new house nicer than the one before. My sister even had her own horse.

I never got on well with school, Chancellor's in Brookmans Park. My grades were quite good, but the whole system didn't really suit me. School teaches you to get your head down, to go and live your life in a certain manner, to fit in, to be

My mum, dad and sister back in the day having it large.

average, to go and work for someone else for fifty years and then retire on a modest pension. I didn't want any of that. No entrepreneur can want any of that.

I had a group of mates but the two I got on best with were Jonna and Darryl. Darryl pretty much became part of my family. We were never in the same form or sets at school – he didn't end up passing any of his exams – but we became best mates from the moment we met.

With Darryl and Jonna I could have a laugh. I hated school but there was the odd moment of light relief. I've always been a prankster. There were knee knocks, pantsings, bridges formed behind people so they would fall over, chairs pulled from classmates as they were about to sit down. Then, one day, came the moment I'd been waiting for. For over a year, I'd kept an electric shock pen in my pencil case.

'Has anyone got a pen I can borrow?' asked my teacher, Dr. Nafu.

My moment had finally arrived.

I leapt up and handed him my electric shock pen with a broad smile on my face.

Later that day I was excluded from school.

Back then I didn't want to be a prankster or an entertainer. I loved playing jokes on people, but my every waking hour was spent trying to become a footballer. Break and lunchtimes at school were dedicated to the sport. We'd always play a game in the playground called bumslaps. It was essentially a shooting game, but whoever lost then had to bend over in front of the cage and get the ball blasted at their bum by all the other players.

Playing football earnt me credibility at school. And that credibility soon went

through the roof when I signed for the academy of my local professional club, Luton Town.

It was the first step on the pathway to my dream. Training sessions were held twice a week, with a match every Sunday against another academy side. My team was made up of the best young players in the local area, playing against the best young players in the whole country.

It should have been everything I ever wanted. Yet every week that negativity crept in.

What if I make a mistake?

What if I don't win the first tackle?

What if I don't impress the coach?

Everything was 'what if?' It was the way I was tuned in. 'An optimist turns that 'what if' into a positive, an 'I will'. I will make an amazing pass. I will score a couple of goals today. I will impress the coach. But I just couldn't get into that mindset.

When you always see negativity, when you're convinced that something bad is coming around the corner, then you'll be right. Negativity breeds negativity.

I first met Woody when I was in my teens. He'd befriended my cousin Adam and the two of them were close. Woody started coming to our family events. So did Darryl.
The two of us used to spend hours playing football with Adam and Woody under the street lamps.
Kerbie, Wembley, Donkey, Flicks –

CHAPTER 4
WINNERS AND LOSERS

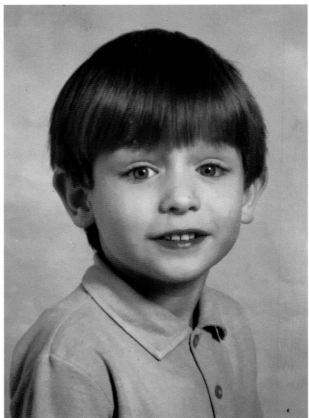

CHAPTER 4

WINNERS AND LOSERS

Woody: I had a tough upbringing as a kid. The exact opposite of Kleiny and his comfortable life. Things happened back then that impacted me deeply. And what did I do? I swept all those things under a rug, blocked them out and hoped I hid them well enough.

My parents split up when I was four.

Swept under the rug.

My mum was diagnosed as bipolar.

Swept under the rug.

She ran onto the pitch during one of my football games because the police wouldn't let her see me due to her mental health issues.

Swept under the rug.

That should have been a beautiful moment. She broke the law because she was so desperate to see me. With

With Diego Maradona while shooting In The Hands of the Gods.

It was at this time that Adam – and, by extension, his cousin Kleiny – came into my life.

Then, a big break arrived. I was to be one of five football freestylers that made up the cast of a movie documentary called In the Hands of the Gods. The idea behind the film was that we'd busk our way from the UK to Argentina to meet our hero, Diego Maradona.

Guess what? We did it. When I met Maradona I crumbled. It was such a big moment in my life. My self-belief rocketed as a result. The journey in

the film was anything but easy, so the fact that I managed to do it, after going through hell and back, really made me believe that I could do anything. It was in my power to go out and get anything I wanted in life. All that mattered was how far I was prepared to go.

None of us could have guessed how successful the film was going to be. In our minds, we were just football tricksters who blagged our way across the world to meet our hero. Yet all of a sudden we were at the Cannes Film Festival with hundreds of people watching us on screen. Jude

Rehearsing at Wembley Stadium infront of 90,000 empty seats.

Law, Jessica Simpson, Cesc Fabregas, there were all kinds of movie stars and athletes not just watching our film, but standing up and giving us an ovation. A red carpet Leicester Square premiere followed – though they changed the red carpet for green astroturf just for us – a few months later. It was absolutely surreal, one of the biggest natural highs of my life. For a small snippet of time I lived like a Hollywood superstar.

And then it was over. The realisation hit me the morning after the premiere. I woke up in my apartment to discover the high had disappeared. Instead, I felt low, almost depressed that my surreal experiences were going to be over.

It was a mad rollercoaster of emotion to have gone through.

I'd got the bug. I wanted to ride the rollercoaster again. All of those

Hollywood style experiences inspired me to find the next natural high, to achieve success again.

In The Hands of the Gods went on to become the UK's widest release of a movie documentary at the time, and the third biggest in the world. While all that was happening my freestyling went from strength to strength...

A client I was working with in Switzerland asked me to work as a UEFA skills expert. It involved presenting to camera and then providing a tutorial of how to do a specific skill. And then I partnered with Kleiny, which was when things really took off. We went on Britain's Got Talent, did well, and got a lot of credibility within the industry. Kleiny joined me as a UEFA skills expert, our first experience of presenting as a double act to camera. The buzz was unreal.

I saw Kleiny's rise as a freestyler, but I then saw his fall when everything happened to him in those couple of months. It was horrible to see his breakdown. And all the while I never realised how close I was to heading down a similar path.

That's the problem with sweeping things under the rug: you never fully hide them. And they build up.

I was silenced by my past. Nobody knew what I'd been through because I hadn't told a soul. I was used to just getting on and coping.

Which is the most dangerous thing you can do.

When you're silenced you're not in control of certain things. And when you have a drink or two of alcohol, you're not always in control of yourself.

Parts of the past that I had thought were long buried started to come out when I went drinking. They bubbled to the top and took hold of my emotions, haunting my every movement.

Someone I was out with could do the tiniest little thing and I'd react badly. I could get aggressive, upset, or even retreat inside myself. It made me feel like the whole world was against me.

When I wasn't drinking I was fairly stable. But when I had a few drinks in me I became a different person. And in those darkest of times, when the past truly caught up with me, I wondered if enough was enough. If I should find a way out of it all.

Sometimes I was reckless.

Sometimes I was plain stupid. I put myself in danger and didn't care if I lived or died. A moving car. Train tracks. A roundabout.

My actions were hurting those closest to me.

I needed to find a solution before something truly bad happened.

That's when Kleiny told me The Secret.

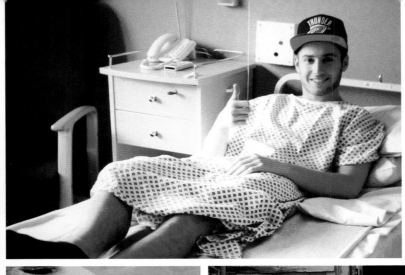

CHAPTER 5
THE
SECRET

CHAPTER 5

THE SECRET

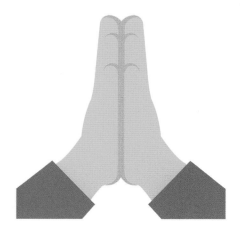

Kleiny: The Secret is based around the law of attraction. It states that the body is a magnet where your thoughts can have a direct impact on your life. If you're feeling positive then you'll attract more positivity into your life. The flip side of that is negative feelings bring more negativity into your life.

Take it back to what I'd been feeling up to that point in my life. Before Darryl introduced me to The Secret, I'd always been a negative person. That brought more negativity. I was always convinced something bad was around the corner. The Secret spoke to me straight away.

Thoughts become things.

If you're feeling positive, you'll think positive. If you think positive, positive things will happen. They'll become your reality.

Woody: I used to suffer from being overly cautious. Some people may call it realism. If I had a Plan A then I'd make a Plan B. It was all about being careful, making sure that if we're doing thing X over here then thing Y might happen and so we'd better have an alternative option.

The Secret tells you not to do that. If you're putting the idea out into the universe that your Plan A won't work then it won't. You need to have complete faith in your plan. If you get rid of what might happen then there's no way that it will happen.

Having a get-out plan before you even start something is dangerous.

Will Smith says it best. He never has a Plan B because it's just a distraction from Plan A.

Kleiny: The most successful people all live their life by The Secret, even if they don't realise it. They believe in themselves.

That's not to say that negative thoughts never creep in. But when you live your life by The Secret, you learn to remove those negative thoughts from your mind as quickly as possible.

I watched the film of The Secret, read the book, then I took the principles it lays out and applied them to my own life. How could I turn the negative things that had happened into a positive?

Losing all of the family money? It gave me a passion and desire that maybe wasn't there before.

Injuring my back? It put me onto an entertainment pathway. The Secret taught me to see that back injury in a positive light. Looking back now, it's the best thing that ever happened to me. If I hadn't injured my back then I probably wouldn't be writing this book right now. I'd still be working as a football freestyler and there'd be no WAKpack. Nobody would be that interested in my story.

Woody: Even in the most extreme cases, you can take a positive from a negative. Lose a loved one? Maybe their departure stopped them from suffering. That's a positive. So's the fact that when you come out the other side you find that you're a stronger person. You dealt with something that's unbelievably painful.

That's how I had to see the stuff that had scarred me. The positive was that I'd come through it all and made it out the other side.

Whatever happened to me after that, no matter how bad, I knew there was a light on the other side. There is nothing that I can't get over. My past has made me the person I am today. And you know what? I wouldn't change any of it.

Kleiny: We all go through hard times. The difference between leading a happy life and a sad one is how you deal with those hard times. You're going to have bad times, sad times, all kinds of negative emotions – The Secret doesn't deny that – but by altering your mindset you can change your life.

Woody: Just like we did.

Kleiny: After being introduced to The Secret, my panic attacks went. I started to believe in myself, to speak positively and to remove all negativity from my life. Some friends and family members disappeared out of my life as a result. I couldn't surround myself with negativity. Suddenly everything seemed more manageable.

Woody: Look to your left. Look to your right. The people surrounding you are the ones who are going to drive you. Some people are scared by success. They're the overly cautious ones. And they're the ones who aren't going to help you achieve your dreams.

Kleiny: One of the most important tools of The Secret is visualisation. You could call it imagination. Close your eyes and think of something you want. Imagine yourself getting it. That's visualisation. Imagine yourself achieving it. That's manifestation.

Once you put that thought out into the universe it creates positive energy. Watch it happen over and over again in your head. Then achieve it.

Your vision could be anything. It could be money, fame or even just health. I wanted to make something of myself. I didn't want to stay in my small flat for my whole life, tying shoelaces for children in my job as a school sport coach. I enjoyed the job, but it wasn't my dream. I felt there was more out there for me.

Woody: Again, to take a positive, working as a school sport coach gave us an amazing grounding in life. I also had my own coaching business. I still have it now. Grafting every day, tying children's shoelaces, it made us appreciate what it is to work. Public speaking, treating others with respect, confidence – they're all skills I've learnt from coaching.

Darryl: Me and Kleiny used to drive to coaching sessions together. 'Close your eyes,' I'd tell him. 'Imagine we're not in this old banger. Imagine it's a Range Rover.' Maybe I shouldn't have told him that while he was driving!

Kleiny: It wasn't just the Range Rover I was visualising. I pictured being massive on YouTube, sharing videos to millions

of followers, working as a TV presenter. To make the visions even more realistic, I made a list. Since that moment, I've been ticking points off that list.

Get a million followers ✓

Buy a Mercedes ✓

Live in a mansion ✗

Receive a cheque for £5 million ✗

The last one is an idea from Jim Carrey. I could already picture the cheque and wanted that vision to be with me at all times. So I wrote myself a cheque for £5 million and put it in my wallet. It's all to do with your mindset. Even if you haven't got something, you have to believe you have. If you can see it in your mind then you can hold it in your hand.

Woody: We started a series of sketches where we threw each other's wallets and phones into swimming pools. That cheque meant so much to Kleiny. I had to plead with him to take it out of his wallet so that it didn't get soaked. Eventually he placed it on his vision board for me.

Kleiny: The £5 million cheque was so clear in my mind. So was the YouTube success. And it was the same with Woody and Darryl. Even though we were spending all hours of the day creating content, investing all of our money for just hundreds of views, we knew that it was just a matter of time before we made it big.

If you put that positive thought out into the universe, the universe will soon deliver for you.

Woody: It won't happen straight away. Even the people who look like they've had their success overnight – those who have won The X Factor, for instance – have had to work for it. They've been slaving away for years, practising in their bedrooms, busking on the street, playing in pubs.

Some ambitions can come more quickly through believing, whereas others take time.

Kleiny: I want £5 million tomorrow.

Woody: That's not going to happen.

But by tomorrow you can put the tools in place to start you on your journey to getting £5 million. Then every time you travel on the journey to £5 million, you increase your chances of success.

To put that in the context of our own social-media journey: by putting out regular content we knock on the door of success. Every time we travel up the path and knock on that door, our success gets a bit closer. By staying visible online and staying positive in person, we will get wherever we want to go or do whatever we choose.

Kleiny: I already believe we're the world's biggest entertainers. I believe we're as big as Ant and Dec. It's not just talking about it; it's truly believing it. When you adopt that mindset, you enter a room and have the attitude that everyone there knows you already.

And even back when we were grafting for 129 views, I still believed that we were the world's biggest entertainers.

Woody: That's The Secret.

CHAPTER 6
MAN
DOWN

CHAPTER 6

MAN DOWN

Kleiny: Not everyone gets The Secret. Not everyone always shares the same vision.

Woody: We were sold on it immediately though. Yes, we were grafting, but we knew what we were grafting for.

Kleiny: Harry may not have seen the vision. What he could definitely see was that we were all grafting a crazy amount of hours for no return.

Woody: He's an artist. A true creative. But he didn't necessarily have the same drive for our new project.

Kleiny: We talk a lot about upbringing. Harry's was similar to mine. His dad runs a painting and decorating business and must be a millionaire. Anything Harry wanted, he was given. Where us Kleins lost all our money, Harry's family held onto theirs. He's a great lad, a really good mate, but

that easy upbringing maybe made it harder for him to understand our mindset.

Woody: At first he was coming up with great ideas. He brought a lot to the table. But as time went on he became less and less involved. The situation wasn't for him. We could see that, and one day I sat him down. 'Don't be obliged to be part of this,' I told him, 'At the end of the day you have to live your life and do what pleases you. If that's not this then so be it. Just be honest with us.' I could tell he was relieved. He told me the direction he wanted to go in, that it was different to where we were heading. 'I can't do it, Woods,' he told me.

Can't.

It's not a word in our vocabulary.

Kleiny: So four became three.

Woody: It didn't shake our vision one bit.

Kleiny: When I heard the news, I just thought: 'He's missing out. He'll kick himself.'

Woody: In theory, Harry's decision meant Darryl had to start pulling his weight - and not just from behind the camera.

Darryl: One day Kleiny phoned me up. 'Daz,' he said. 'This isn't me being horrible, but what are you actually doing for us? You've got 15 per cent of the business. Why do you deserve that? What are you doing right now? Playing Xbox.'

Well, yeah, I was playing Xbox when he called me.

'Do something for us,' he replied. 'You've got an amazing opportunity. Put some work in and show us you're worth something to us. Make yourself important. Can you do more?'

'Yeah,' I replied.

But in my head I was saying: 'Shut up, Kleiny. Leave me alone.' I didn't need all of the stress he was giving me. Especially when I already had the stress of being 2-0 down at the time he phoned.

Kleiny: How were you 2-0 down? I can't believe you ever lost a game of FIFA when you spent so much time on the Xbox.

Darryl: Because you were putting me off! But seriously, Xbox used to be a daily routine for me. I'd come home from my coaching sessions and turn on FIFA, then that was me done for the day. If I didn't need to film, then I switched off and didn't give a second thought to Woody, Kleiny or our project.

That phone call turned out to be a real kick up the backside.

I carried on playing Xbox for the rest of the night, but then I woke up the next day with Kleiny's words still in my ear.

How was playing Xbox going to help me in the future?

It wasn't. I realised that I was getting in from my day job and just wasting time until it was time to go back for the next coaching session.

The next evening I didn't turn on the Xbox. I went on YouTube and started researching.

Kleiny said I should be working my nuts off to prove my value.

Kleiny: And that's what he did.

Woody: He worked so hard that he made himself indispensable. Within a few months, Darryl impressed us so much that he not only proved he should be earning his 15 per cent, but potentially a whole lot more.

Kleiny: Sometimes we all need a kick up the butt.

Darryl: Instead of the Xbox, I got in and watched other creators' content. What were they doing? Which of their videos worked? Which didn't? How could we use their ideas and put our own spin on them?

Kleiny: Will Smith says that when you're looking to be successful you should look at others who have been successful and imitate, then innovate.

Imitate.

Then innovate.

Woody: If you want to be the best, you need to learn from the best. Research has always been a big part of what we do. Darryl turned himself around, made himself irreplaceable by putting in the hours. His input became so important to us. Kleiny's also good at finding the time to see what others are doing. That's how we work as a team. Which, after Harry departed, is exactly what we were. A team with one less person – a man down – but a team that shared the same mindset.

Kleiny: And that's The Secret.

Surround yourself with people of the same mindset. It changes everything.

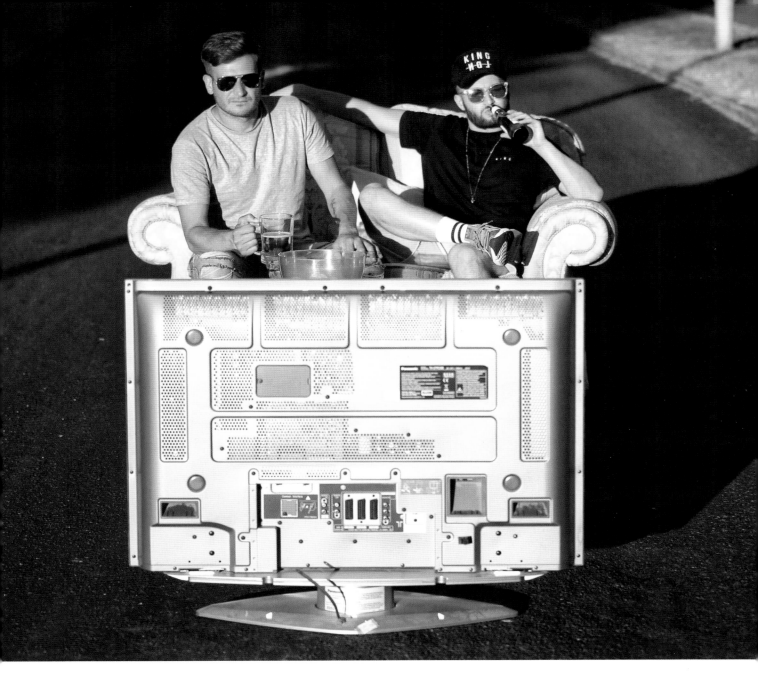

you can justify the title, you can get away with it.

Kleiny: So now we had our title, and we had our group message list. The next part of the strategy was choosing an appropriate thumbnail. For those who don't know, a thumbnail is a still image that shows up to preview your video. It could appear on the trending page, related videos or recommended next videos. As with the title, the more interesting the thumbnail, the better. You have to make viewers want to know more about the thumbnail and click play to find out rather than scroll past it.

Woody: The best ones are full of emotion. You can't be half-hearted with your expressions. This is where Kleiny comes into his own. He's always been super-critical when it comes to thumbnails. We could have shot the most perfect photo, our facial expressions exactly how we wanted them, and Kleiny could say: 'It's not right, let's do it again. This time, let's move your hat so it's coming off at this angle instead of the angle in the photo we've just taken. It'll make it more dramatic.' Kleiny orders us back into position, moves my hat about three centimetres and takes the photo again.

No detail was too small for our new strategy. Those three centimetres could be the difference between going viral and not.

Everything was geared towards making something that was perfect into something even better than perfect.

Kleiny: We had keywords too. When you upload a video to YouTube you choose the right keywords to help your content become more discoverable. The same with hashtags. They help your video become more prominent with the algorithm. Again, this came down to research. Which hashtags were trending? Which could we use to get our content seen?

Woody: Descriptions as well. They're another way of encouraging people to watch your content as well as engaging those who have already watched it.

Kleiny: Of all the new pieces of strategy, engagement was the most important. The best way of increasing engagement was to write a comment in the comment section of our video. YouTube lets you pin the comment to the top of the feed, so our comment was the first everyone would see.

@WoodyandKleiny: Hey guys, thanks for watching. What would you like to see in our next video?

Woody: People saw those comments and it encouraged them to comment on the video with what they'd like to see. The more comments on the video, the more likely it could go viral.

We then replied to every comment.

Every single comment.

At first it wasn't hard to do because our videos would get about three comments. As the strategy had more of an effect, however, the comments started coming.

Having fun whilst filming

THE BEST PAUSE
CHALLENGE ON THE...

13:56

HILARIOUS PLASTIC BALL
PRANK!! (priceless reactions)

4:07

INSANE EXPLODING
WATERMELON...

6:17

Kleiny: We all took pride in replying to every comment. That's because every comment meant so much to us. To have someone who had not only invested the time to watch our video, but to also tell us about it, was amazing. The numbers weren't massive, but we still saw everyone who commented as our own loyal fanbase. By replying to their comments, all we were doing was showing them a bit of love and thanking them for investing that time.

Woody: When you reply to a comment, you turn a follower into a fan. If they comment on another of your videos and you reply again, they become a superfan. The next time you reply to them, they go from a superfan to a soldier ready to go to war with you.

If someone is negative in the comments – maybe suggesting something is fake – then the soldiers jump to defend you. 'Go somewhere else,' they say, 'you don't say those things here.' It soon became a movement. They weren't just fans, nor even soldiers. They were the #WAKpack.

Every single follower means so much to us. Yes, it's a bit of a cliché, but we know what it's like to be able to count all of your followers on one hand. We know the graft that's needed to gain a follower. And we know that without our followers we're nothing.

Kleiny: Without our followers we wouldn't be writing this book.

Woody: It's the same philosophy that comes with those three centimetres. Look after the small things and the bigger things will take care of themselves.

Kleiny: The smaller things were being looked after. And the bigger things?

Woody: Well, oh my god, you're not going to believe what happened next!

CHAPTER 8
SUNDAY– NOT ALWAYS A DAY OF REST

CHAPTER 8

SUNDAY— NOT ALWAYS A DAY OF REST 😴

Woody: We created our YouTube page on 30 March 2013. That was our main focus, and we also created pages on all of the other social-media platforms.

'Kleins,' I asked, 'where do we want to be big?'

'We want to be a powerhouse,' he replied. 'Forget just YouTube. We need to be big in every possible area we can.'

At first that was YouTube and Twitter.

We created Facebook and Instagram accounts too, but they weren't so important at the time.

Darryl: By 6 December 2014 we had 269 followers on Instagram.

Kleiny: Get in there!

Woody: Back then, Instagram wasn't really a platform for creators. You

could share photos and that was it. Then a few months later, video was introduced to the platform. There were major limitations though. Videos could only be fifteen seconds long and had no view metrics.

We still put some content on Instagram and Facebook, but YouTube was the most important place to upload videos.

Kleiny: And then one of our videos banged. On Facebook.

Woody: The share button on Facebook meant that there were opportunities to grow. Taking it back to the 256 people on our group message list: imagine each one of them had an average of a hundred friends. If they all shared it on their Facebook pages, that video would be seen 25,600 times. Yes, it's popped up on their timeline randomly and the people watching the video don't necessarily know who we are,

but if all hundred friends of each person sharing the video like it and share it again then the video would be seen... well, a lot of times! It's the domino effect.

Kleiny: That domino effect worked to our advantage. Blood, sweat and tears had gone into growing our YouTube channel for little return. All of a sudden we had a bit of luck on Facebook – and boom!

One million views.

Woody: One million views.

Kleiny: I couldn't believe it when it happened. All those years for nothing on YouTube and then we suddenly blew up on Facebook.

Woody: Is that a tear in your eye?

Kleiny: 20 September 2015. Our first million-view video.

Woody: And it wasn't even on our page. It was posted by UNILAD. We were tagged in the post, though, so it still helped our page grow massively.

Kleiny: The video was called 'Sunday League Stereotypes'. It was pure football comedy based on what we'd experienced from playing grassroots football. There was a scene with everyone shouting at the linesman; we had the oranges at half-time; the guy who wears his socks over his knees and thinks he's Cristiano Ronaldo... I know the clue is in the title but the video was just showing all of the proper stereotypes you see.

Woody: I was at my apartment on the day it happened. It was a Sunday and my dad had popped round for something or other.

I opened my laptop and loaded Facebook.

My heart skipped a beat.

'Look, Dad, come look at this!'

Dad came over and I explained everything to him, how we'd made a video and it'd been picked up and posted and was now blowing up and it was crazy and just look at those views and oh wow look how many new likes our Facebook page was getting. Getting a hundred new likes on Facebook was a big deal for us before that video.

Every time I clicked refresh, our page had more likes and the video had a crazy amount more views.

'Woah, son,' he said, dead impressed.

By now the video had been seen 750,000 times on UNILAD. Five minutes later I clicked refresh and it had hit 800,000 views.

Woody's Dad popped over before the million

Kleiny: The first time I saw the video it was on 700,000 views.

Wow.

Refresh.

730,000.

Refresh.

750,000.

I'm seriously gassed. Darryl's next to me going: 'We're going to hit a million.' He's saying it over and over again.

We're going to hit a million.

We're going to hit a million.

I ran home and opened up my laptop. It was getting closer and closer. Then we hit a million and it was crazy. I was in my room dancing and singing to 'A Milli' by Lil Wayne. Literally, crazy, all the time thinking to myself: 'Wow, this works. The Secret works.'

So many hours had been spent manifesting a video with a million views. Now it had happened.

Woody: That video gave us validation. Friends and family started to recognise we were on to something. Others reached out to us to say they'd seen our video.

We could enjoy our success, but we couldn't just make one viral piece of content then put our feet up and make a cup of tea.

Now we knew the feeling of success. We'd tasted that feeling and we liked it. We had to do it again. As soon as we could.

Kleiny: We'd hit the wave. It came from nowhere, and now we had to ride it as hard as possible for as long as possible. The only option was to put YouTube on ice and go after Facebook.

Woody: What was the answer? We sat down as a three and racked our brains for our next viral video. After hours of thought, we landed on an idea that used up every ounce of creativity we had.

'Sunday League Stereotypes 2'.

Things that always happen at Sunday league football.

36.2K Likes   9.8K Comments   2M Views

CHAPTER 10
PLEASE DON'T TAKE ME HOME

CHAPTER 10

PLEASE DON'T TAKE ME HOME

Woody: £2,000.

Kleiny: £2,000. It felt like £1 million.

Darryl: When Agent Dan told us that he'd got us a job for a major alcohol brand that would pay £2,000, we couldn't believe it. 'I can see the finish line,' I remember saying to Woody. 'We're getting so close. So many brands are going to work with us now. Fame is just around the corner.'

I couldn't have been more wrong.

The £2,000 really went to my head. And we weren't even getting £2,000. The money was being split between the three of us! That's £666.66 each.

Woody: Three years and three months for two grand.

Kleiny: We were absolutely buzzing. Then we found out the details of the job and honestly couldn't have

CHAPTER 11
THE WAK TRANSFOR-MATION

CHAPTER 11

THE WAK TRANSFOR-MATION

Woody: Add it all up. We've got our first million-view video, our own agent, our first paid brand deal. You'd have thought it'd be all plain sailing, right? Me and Darryl certainly did. But Kleiny suggested otherwise.

Kleiny: I first brought it up the night before we left for Ibiza. We were all sitting round in my apartment, having a laugh and looking forward to our first paid job. Woody and Darryl were so excited, saying how this was the start of a new beginning, the first step on the path to millions.

Then I told them what I thought: 'We're not going in the right direction.'

I'd been considering it for weeks. When we first started our YouTube page, we were some of the only creators to be putting out football comedy content. Now more and more were getting involved. It was becoming a saturated market. And not only that, but by

CHAPTER 12
AMERICAN DREAM

CHAPTER 12

AMERICAN DREAM

Welcome to Hollywood. What's your dream? Everybody comes here. This is Hollywood. Land of dreams. Some dreams come true. Some don't. But keep on dreaming. This is Hollywood. Always time to dream, so keep on dreaming.

Kleiny: Woody, will you stop playing that speech from Pretty Woman?

Darryl: We're not even in LA.

Woody: Alright, alright.

Kleiny: It's become his trademark. Any time LA comes up, Woody is straight onto that Pretty Woman scene.

Woody: It's a good speech.

Kleiny: It is, to be fair. The first time Woody played it we were all absolutely buzzing. You know why? Because we were on our way to Hollywood.

have a clue who he was so I kept declining him.

Woody: We had to rely on Cornell to film us at VidCon. Darryl wasn't exactly devastated.

Darryl: 'What a shame,' I remember saying to them, all the while planning what fun I could have instead of filming.

Kleiny: We managed to get Darryl into VidCon on the final day. Woody took him up to security at the venue and claimed that Darryl had lost his pass. Darryl gave them the puppy-dog eyes and Woody pleaded for them to let him in. 'It's the last day, he's been to all of the other days,' he promised. 'His name is Paul Klein.'

Little did they know that Paul Klein was already in the building. The security

staff bought it and Darryl made his way in, meaning there were two Paul Kleins in VidCon on that final day.

Woody: We were so desperate and broke that we had to beg Darryl to be let into VidCon. Fast-forward three years and our situation has changed completely.

How did the change come about? Because LA filled us with knowledge. We gained so much insight and so much good advice that we flew back to England brimming with creativity. The fire to become the world's biggest creators had long since been ignited. But the LA experience turned that fire into a forest fire. We were burning to make our dreams happen.

And we were desperate to go back to LA as soon as possible.

CHAPTER 14
CAN IT SWIM?

CHAPTER 14

CAN IT SWIM?

Kleiny: 250,000 followers on Instagram. 600,000 likes on Facebook. It was mad progress since our first LA trip. We were sure that the way to make the next step up was to return to LA.

Darryl: We all thought it was so inspirational how we'd gone from almost no followers on Instagram to 250,000 in just under a year. Little did we know what was to come.

Kleiny: It had been a year of rapid growth and learning. The no-football strategy was working. Most of our followers didn't even know we'd done football content. Then there were those who had mocked us and laughed behind our backs. Those same people were now asking us to record congratulatory messages for their own companies and personalised shout-out videos for their loved ones.

Woody: There are lots of fickle people in the world. We know who they are,

and we know who the people are who have supported us from day one.

Kleiny: With extra growth comes extra responsibility. When you're making content for 10,000 people you can take shortcuts. You can rely on Darryl to film, and then try and edit out the blur. With more followers comes more pressure. You simply have to produce for them. In LA the second time, we wanted to go hard on the filming. Darryl was still going to have a camera with him, but we needed a professional cameraman to help us make the most of the opportunities that were coming our way. And what opportunities they were! We'd spent months DMing creators and searching

for collaborations. Now that we had a notable following of our own, we were being taken more seriously, and the fact that we were from England also went in our favour. We lined up filming sessions with C-Lo, Dre Day Durham, Jessenia and Piques.

Woody: We were buzzing to shoot with Piques. He's the OG, one of the guys Kleiny had told us to imitate and then innovate from.

Kleiny: We'd been watching his content for years as fans, so imagine how we felt to be shooting with him.

Woody: And imagine how frustrated we'd have been if Darryl was shooting.

You can't shoot content with Piques only for it to be out of focus!

Kleiny: I pushed hard for us to bring along a mate of mine from school, Jonna. He was working on shows like Gold Rush at the time and was also doing plenty for the Discovery Channel. He was quickly developing a reputation for himself within the industry and was immensely talented. I knew he could help us smash LA.

Again, it was a case of spending money we didn't have, of speculating to accumulate.

And it almost didn't work out.

Once Darryl and Woody had okayed a professional cameraman, I phoned Jonna.

I didn't realise that he'd just broken up with his girlfriend of seven years. Nor did I realise that he was just about to travel round Thailand by himself. When I say 'just about', I mean he was literally on the internet and booking his flight to Thailand when my call came through.

'Bro, we're going to LA,' I told him. 'We're looking to film hard. We can't do it with Darryl alone. Are you up for it?'

I sold Jonna the dream because I knew how important it was for him to come out with us. He's a talented guy. Amazing at filming but also capable of directing and shooting photos. And he'd been to LA plenty of times to shoot content. He knew all the spots to go to.

I'd caught Jonna at a good time. He loves a laugh and loves a holiday with the lads. Most importantly, he believed in our vision. He knew the effect social media would soon have on the world.

Jonna: LA was eye-opening. I've known Woody, Kleiny and Darryl for

years. But it wasn't until I travelled to LA with them that I realised the extent of their struggle. The social-media game isn't an easy one. For every creator who gains a following, hundreds of thousands fail. Woody, Kleiny and Darryl all knew that and so they ploughed as much of their time into their social channels as possible. Nothing was off limits.

Flying to LA to shoot content sounds like a dream. The reality was different. All of their followers saw the amazing videos we created. They didn't see Woody, Kleiny and Darryl waking up at 7am every day to post videos and reply to comments. Do you know why they did that? Because they analysed everything and found out that the window between 7am and 9am was the best time to upload. They had to work so hard that they barely even got to see any of LA. If I wanted to go out, I could only usually rely on Darryl to come with me. On the rare occasions that the whole team went out for a drink, there'd still be the knock on the door in the morning from Kleiny at 7am on the dot. It'd always be the same.

'Woody, Woody. I've just uploaded the video. You need to get on the comments, lad.'

Woody would roll over, barely functioning. 'Yeah, yeah, sure,' he'd say, opening his phone and typing away with one eye still closed.

Woody: Yes, there was struggle. But we had to struggle. With every struggle came a breakthrough. And having Jonna come to LA with us was our next breakthrough. When he came on board, that was the moment that we became proper creators. Until that point we were two guys who had a presence on social media.

Kleiny: The plan was to shoot all of the time. That's why we needed Jonna. It

was going to be an intense trip but we knew it's what we had to do.

The five of us – me, Woody, Darryl, Jonna and my girlfriend – landed in LA and made it through customs with no difficulty. Woody brought both parts of his driving licence and Jonna also had his. Jonna knew LA so well that he took the wheel and drove us straight to the Airbnb without even using a satnav.

That was when we knew we'd made the right decision to bring him along.

Darryl: We dumped our stuff and headed out to Tim Frasier's local

bar to meet the legend himself. Five minutes in and Woody fell asleep.

Woody: Jet lag.

Kleiny: We had a few drinks with Tim. It was great to catch up with him in person. He'd been over to England a few months earlier and Darryl had driven him for seven hours so he could go and see Stonehenge. Americans love their English history!

Woody: The next day Piques turned up to our Airbnb. We hadn't planned anything in particular with him. He suggested we should just jam and think of something to shoot on the spot.

Kleiny: We were star-struck.

Darryl: He turned up in a BMW i8.

Kleiny: 'This guy is balling!'

Darryl: In the back seat he had a dog that was the size of a bear.

Kleiny: Our first impression was that this was a guy living the life. Then we spoke to him and found out he was a super-cool dude who was super down to earth. He's the OG for a reason.

Woody: So what did we do? We pranked him.

Kleiny: Woody spoke to Piques in the main room while me, Jonna and Darryl went into the other room. 'We've got to prank him,' we told each other. But what could we do?

'I've seen this spoons video online. How about we play against Piques?' Darryl suggested.

'He's the OG. He must have seen it,' I replied. 'There's no way we'll fool him.'

'Well, let's try.'

HOW TO PLAY SPOONS

Spoons is a two-player game. Players take it in turns to hit each other over the head with a spoon. Players are only allowed to hold the spoon in their mouth.

HOW TO PLAY SPOONS (WOODY AND KLEINY VERSION)

Spoons is a three-player game. Player One has no clue about the prank, while everyone else is in on it.

Player One places the spoon in their mouth while Player Two leans over. Player One then strikes Player Two over the back of the head with the spoon. As they are using their mouth, they are unable to generate enough power to hurt Player Two.

Player Two then places the spoon in their mouth and Player One leans over. It's important that Player One leans over enough so they are unable to see what is happening. Player Two leans back as if for a normal strike, but when they then move forward, Player Three comes in from the side and smacks Player One over the head with a spoon, using their hand. This allows them to generate enough power to hurt Player One.

Player Two returns to position as Player One roars in pain. Player Two then bends down and allows Player One to have their next go. This continues until blood is drawn or a decision is made to reveal the prank to Player One.

Woody: Talk about risks! This guy is so influential within the industry and we decided to take absolute liberties with him. And this was before getting to know what he was like. We only had our first impression to go off. It was one of those do-or-die moments. It could have gone either way. But we were confident that – if we got it right – our risk could pay off and the video could go viral.

Kleiny: We got Woody in the room and told him the plan. The next step was to tee it up so Piques would want to play. It was decided that Darryl and Jonna would go into the main room and randomly start playing the two-player version of Spoons. This, we theorised, would interest Piques so much that he'd ask to play.

In Darryl and Jonna went. Straight away Piques was onto it. 'Yo, what are you doing? That looks fun. Can I play?'

Heh heh heh.

Darryl passed his spoon to Piques, who then placed it in his mouth.

'You should play against Woody first,' Darryl suggested. 'He's the champion. Honestly, I've never seen him beaten. He can't be beaten!'

'Okay,' Piques said. 'Hey, we should film this.'

Heh heh heh.

Piques went first and obviously his shot barely tickled Woody's head.

'You're getting the hang of this,' we encouraged from the side.

Then it was Woody's turn. Piques bent over and Woody leant back as if for a normal strike. As he transferred his weight forward, I came from the side and cracked Piques over the head.

'AAAARRRRRGGGGGGHHHHHH!!!'

Piques screamed in pain. He couldn't work out how Woody had generated so much power.

'We told you he was the champ,' we explained. 'He's unbeatable. Unbeatable.'

Piques rubbed his head and stood upright, determined to get Woody back. Again, his shot barely tickled Woody's head. And again, I cracked the spoon over Piques's head.

After the fourth or fifth go, with Piques on the verge of concussion, we started to feel bad.

'Hey Piques, check this out.' We showed him the footage.

Do or die.

Sink or swim.

He screamed in rage, then burst into laughter. We laughed along, but deep down we all breathed a collective sigh of relief. Piques loved it and we'd got an amazing video. We knew it'd bang once we put it online.

Woody: That reaction confirmed to us what a sound guy Piques is. He comes from a sporting background and that makes him quite competitive. A sporting background is a bit of an understatement really. He used to play for the same team as Cristiano Ronaldo in the Sporting Lisbon academy. The pair of them were room-mates. That experience means he's always up for a challenge – and also able to win and lose with grace.

Kleiny: From that moment, Piques became our boy. We all got on so well with him. It was lucky he was able to take a prank because he was soon on the end of plenty more.

Woody: Our second LA trip was when our pranks were taken up a level. It was ruthless. Before then we'd always pranked each other. Ever since we'd known each other. But it had always been off camera. The second LA trip was the first time we were really pranking each other just for the camera.

We developed a rule: make sure you film it. If you're on the end of a prank, the first thing you have to ask is whether it was filmed. If it was, you have to accept what happened. If it wasn't, you get to kick the pranker in the shins.

Kleiny: If it wasn't filmed then it was a waste. Don't waste.

Woody: In LA we lived together so there was no escape from the pranks. At any one time there were at least five or six different pranks going on. There was no way you could protect yourself. Darryl reckons he's unprankable – he doesn't even jump when we blow an airhorn in his ear – but me and Kleiny are both jumpy by nature.

The swimming pools, Airbnb and scenic locations made for amazing pranks. Airhorns, knee-knocks, slipper-smashes and phone-catches were all regulars. The biggest of the lot, though, was 'Can It Swim?'

Being around LA swimming pools all the time meant that we could really develop 'Can It Swim?' and create amazing content.

Kleiny: By the end of the trip I was so careful with where all of my belongings were at all times. Anything could get chucked at any moment – the more valuable the better.

Woody: Piques's reaction to the spoons game set a new precedent. If he could take that well, what else could he take well?

'Lads,' I said, 'we need to take this to the next level. Turn the cameras on.'

Piques was strolling around the pool, preparing to shoot a sketch. Kleiny reached over and snatched his phone from the table. 'Aye yo Piques, can your phone swim?'

No no no no no.

Piques looked over and his alarm was evident. He was really panicking.

But we just wanted the shot so badly. Even if we had to buy him a brand-new phone. Speculate to accumulate; short-term loss, long-term gain.

Kleiny launched his phone towards the swimming pool. Piques charged after it and got a hand to it just before it reached the water. It was like he was moving in slow motion. He was swaying, the phone still not yet safe. After a few seconds he steadied himself and started jumping up and down and celebrating.

'Yeahhhhhh!'

Kleiny: That's when Woody came with an 'out of nowhere'. It's a Randy Orton wrestling move that was big at the time. Woody charged at Piques, who was still holding onto his phone but looking in the wrong direction.

Big mistake.

Woody wrapped his arm around Piques's head and dragged him – and his phone – into the water.

It turned out Piques's phone couldn't swim.

That afternoon we went out and bought him a brand-new phone. Piques was so cool about it. He's the OG for a reason.

Woody: We went hard in LA. By the end of our stay we were absolutely drained, both physically and mentally. It had all been worth it. We'd shot some absolute gold that we knew was going to bang. Our success and our vision had never seemed closer or more real. We couldn't wait to make our videos public.

But first it was time to relax and get our energy back. Where better than Las Vegas?

Aye yo Piques; can your phone swim?!

CHAPTER 16
THE TSUNAMI WAVE

CHAPTER 16

THE TSUNAMI WAVE

Woody: We came back from the US with so much footage in the can. Enough to more or less put our feet up until Christmas and enjoy our success while continuing our strategy of posting one video per week, usually across multiple channels. I was happy with that. It took the pressure off and gave me a bit more time to see my family, as well as earn a bit of money from the day job to pay for the LA trip.

Our first upload after LA was our game of spoons with Piques.

It got 2 million views.

Then we uploaded the 'Can It Swim?' video with Piques. That got 4.4 million views.

We'd done it. We hit the wave.

Kleiny: The wave was introduced to us by someone called Zeb Jaffer. Goubtube first put us on to him to

help us build our Facebook following. Zeb is heavily involved with Fortafy Games, which helps give up-and-coming creators massive exposure.

Goub put the three of us into a Facebook group together where we got chatting. After that, the logical next step was to get everyone together on a call. We set it up so everyone from our team could be on the call. Zeb gave us all some positive feedback, told us what was working in his view, and what could be improved, but highlighted how impressed he was with what we were doing.

'Keep doing this. Keep focused. It's coming. It's going to work,' he told us.

'It's just a matter of time before one of your videos hits the wave.'

'What's the wave?'

'The wave can come at any time. It's when a piece of content goes crazy. The views go through the roof, followers jump on your page. The growth is insane. When you hit that wave – and if you keep on doing what you're doing then you will hit it – what you have to do is ride it for as long as possible. Go surfing.'

'What do you mean?'

'I mean when that wave hits, you pump content. Pump it day in, day out. Pump, pump, pump. The wave needs to be fed.'

Woody: That conversation was just before we headed out to LA. And now our video had banged. This had to be the wave. I rang Darryl and Kleiny.

'Boys, we've hit the wave.'
They all agreed. The spoons video was a ripple. The 'Can It Swim?' was a full-blown wave. We'd grown by 30,000 followers overnight.

The excitement levels on that call were crazy. But it wasn't all excitement. The enormity of what was happening to us was creeping in. There was a bit of panic, a case of 'Oh my god, what do we do now?'

Kleiny answered: 'We film. We film every week. We film every day we can possibly film. We edit as much as we film. We keep pumping. We go every single day.'

He was right. We had to ride the wave.

Kleiny: I knew how much Woody loves having videos in the can so I wasn't sure what he was going to say on that call. When he gave us the green light to pump content, I was absolutely buzzing.

I went straight into the edit suite to work on our next set of uploads. We went with a compilation video made up of old footage where we put cling film across doorways as a prank. That got 3.1 million views and truly confirmed that we were now riding the wave. Next up was a 'Stick It In That Old Thing' video. 1.6 million views. Crazy numbers compared to what we were used to.

Woody: There was no time to put our feet up. The day job would have to wait. Whatever time I had left I'd have to squeeze to be with my family. There was no other option. We had to get out there and create more videos.

Kleiny: One you start seeing results, success becomes an addiction.

Woody: Within two weeks we'd used up all of the LA content that was supposed to last us three months. Our growth had gone through the roof. A lot of people were talking about us.

Darryl: We were all over the Explore page on Instagram.

Kleiny: You couldn't miss us.

Woody: We rode that wave and never looked back. Think how long it took us just to get 10,000 followers. Thousands of hours of blood, sweat and tears. Years of bank balances in the red to pay for props and equipment.

And now we'd hit the wave and were gaining thousands of followers each day.

All of a sudden, a million followers had become a real possibility.

Kleiny: We started to see the light at the end of the tunnel. We had 300,000 followers, then in the blink of an eye we had 400,000. Then 500,000. All of those years we'd been manifesting our growth. We always knew it was going to happen, but it's hard to see it when your videos are only getting a hundred views. We had no idea where our growth was going to come from. Now we could see our vision more clearly than ever before.

Hitting a million followers became an inevitability. Woody sent a text message to the rest of the team: 'Let's hit it before Christmas,' he suggested.

Before Christmas.

That was crazy. We needed to hit 7,000 new followers a day. Bear in mind that it had taken us years to reach 7,000 followers. Now we had to do that every single day for just under three months.

But crazy for other people is normal for us. We were manifesting it so much and thinking so positively that 7,000 followers a day seemed a good number. Not only good – achievable.

When you put those positive vibes out into the universe, you know what happens? Positivity comes back around – eventually.

CHAPTER 18
FRIENDS. FAMILY. FRONTLINE.

CHAPTER 18

FRIENDS. FAMILY. FRONTLINE.

Woody: Let me give you another saying: 'There's no "i" in team.' Why do you think there's two of us? And in reality there are far more than just two of us. We contacted Darryl and Harry because we understood we couldn't do it all by ourselves. We needed help.

Over the years the team has continued to grow. There's Agent Dan, Tim Frasier, Jonna, and a few others who haven't yet been mentioned.

From the beginning, we always knew we never wanted to be out there on our own. To reach the scale that we want to reach, you need people helping you. If you've got one person pushing a car it'll only go so far. But with two of you, three of you, four of you all pushing, it'll go a lot further a lot quicker.

Kleiny: We've never built a team for the sake of it. Our team has evolved

CHAPTER 19
THE BIG
1M

CHAPTER 19

THE BIG 1M

Woody: 23 December 2017. The universe rewarded us.

Kleiny: 7,000 new followers every day for three months? It's a little bit too easy...

Woody: I woke up and checked our Instagram page as normal. 999k followers. 'Luce! Luce! It's going to happen.' I kept refreshing the page like a madman, seeing the numbers jump each time. I was so excited. I needed to get up and shower but I didn't want to miss the moment.

When it came, I went absolutely crazy.

Kleiny: I had to go to Hemel Hempstead that morning to pick up some trophies for mine and Darryl's coaching business. Whenever the car stopped I refreshed the page. I couldn't believe it was finally about to happen after all those years of graft.

CHAPTER 20
TABLES ALWAYS TURN

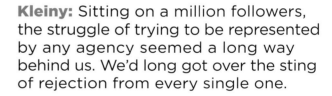

CHAPTER 20

TABLES ALWAYS TURN

Kleiny: Sitting on a million followers, the struggle of trying to be represented by any agency seemed a long way behind us. We'd long got over the sting of rejection from every single one.

Then an email came out of nowhere. One of the only agencies to have had the courtesy to send us a rejection letter wanted to get back in contact with us. This was exactly why we had started our social-media pages up. We knew it was a way of being taken more seriously as TV presenters. We'd manifested it.* And now it was happening.

They wanted to sign us.

After hitting the million, we'd grown rapidly to 1.5 million, then slowed down. Our third LA trip was on the horizon, though, and we knew that would give us the fuel to hit another wave.

We met with the agency a week before heading back to LA. They

---

* Manifestation is a key part of The Secret. You manifest something, picture it happening, and the universe will deliver.

Woody: I've never been more grateful for anything in my life. We still had our LA agency meeting to get to. I didn't want to miss that because Kleiny had driven us off the road.

Jonna: I hold my hands up for that one, boys. I should have kept the keys to myself. But not driving meant that I actually had a chance to relax.

After the success of the previous year, you'd have thought my second LA trip would be easier. That wasn't the case. It's never the case with Woody and Kleiny. If they win, they work even harder to win bigger. And so it was with this LA trip. We worked so hard to make the best-ever content that would go on @WoodyandKleiny.

The 7am wake-up calls returned. Late nights were routine. Kleiny was shut

away in his edit suite for hours on end. He must be the only man to come back from four weeks in the LA sun more pale than when he first left England.

Sometimes he'd emerge from the edit suite with what I thought was a golden piece of content. Then Darryl and Woody would watch it and the three of them would decide it wasn't good enough to post. Other times they'd assess a piece of content that I didn't like too much and decide to go with it. And do you know what? They were usually right.

I could never get the hang of it. The thought and preparation that went into every single piece of content uploaded was crazy.

Woody: Those are the lengths you have to go if you want to be successful. That's why we thought nothing of driving four hours to get a single picture that we may or may not have used for our channels. One day Piques drove us two hours into the desert and two hours back to LA just because he didn't have much on. He didn't ask us for anything. It was all just for love.

Kleiny: One of the pictures was at Runyon Canyon. Otherwise known as The Hottest Place I've Ever Been To. You have to walk up this massive hill to get there, and we decided to do it with two massive suitcases so we could change into different outfits. That way we'd have options when deciding which picture to post.

There we were, walking up this massive hill in our jeans and t-shirts, both lugging massive suitcases, while tourists all around were in their skimpy jogging gear. We were sweating buckets and getting a few funny looks.

'The hotel is up the top, right?' we'd ask a few of the tourists, just for banter.

Darryl lasted about ten minutes before calling it a day.

'This is ridiculous. You boys go on and I'll stay with the suitcases,' he suggested as if it were the noble thing to do. In reality he was just knackered.

Woody: I think he just wanted another chance to check his Instagram. Him and Jonna had both created profiles for the trip and were competing to see who could get the most followers.

Manager Darryl: I was getting so much momentum with my Instagram. I was on fire that trip.

Woody: You were getting at least ten new followers a day.

Kleiny: You might have to wait a little while for a big agency to come calling for you...

Woody: When we met the agency in their LA office they pretty quickly scooted over the fact that Darryl had started his Instagram page. Instead, they showed us round and summarised once more all the different ways they could help us. We were impressed, to say the least.

Ultimately, though, we're loyal to the people who have been loyal to us. Agent Dan had been with us since we had hardly any followers. We didn't want any deal to step on his toes. Agent Dan ran a much smaller business. He couldn't devote all his time to us and had to work with other creators. His business had no special TV arm, no special PR department. It was just him really.

This agency would open up opportunities that Agent Dan might struggle to.

We brought up the subject with them.

'Not possible,' they said. 'If you go with us, we have to be exclusive. We can't work with any other agents or agencies.'

All of a sudden, we had a decision to make.

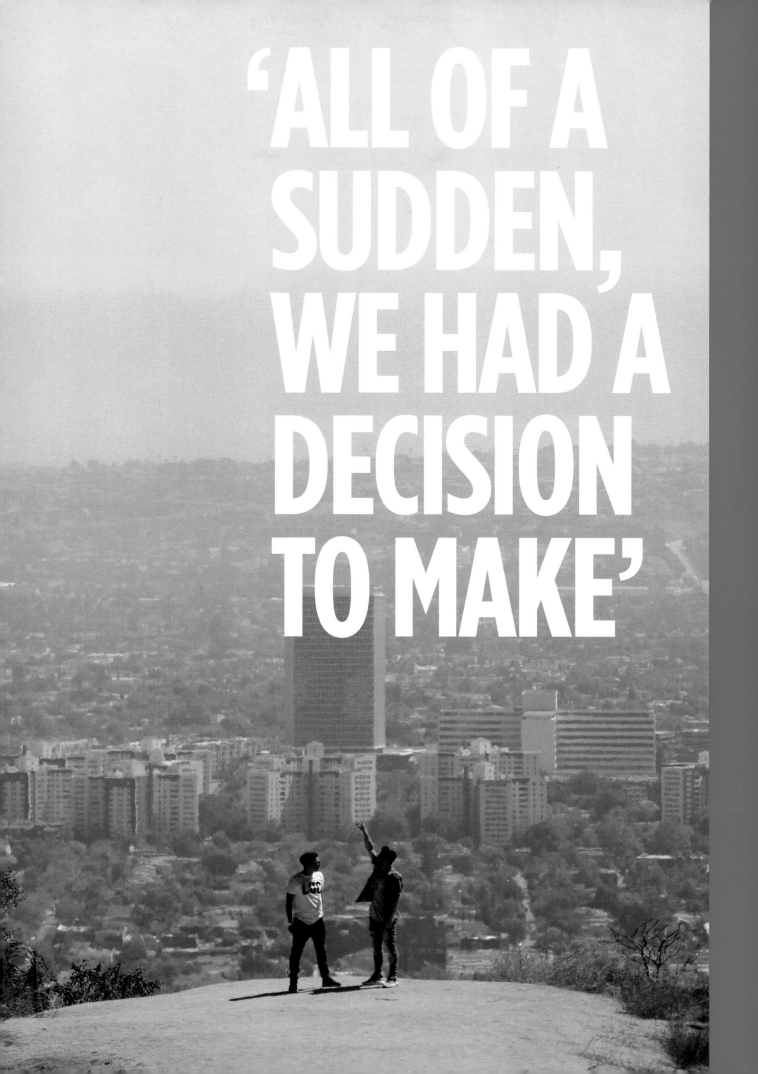

CHAPTER 21
LUC: LET US CREATE

CHAPTER 21

LUC: LET US CREATE

LUC
LET US CREATE

Kleiny: After four weeks of working in LA I was mentally and physically exhausted. So exhausted, in fact, that I ended up being quite ill when I got back to England.

Woody: You were ill because you missed me. I stayed out in LA for another two weeks with Bailey and Lucy. Kleiny didn't know which way to turn without me in the same country.

Kleiny: Yeah, something like that. I was tucked up in bed for a week. I didn't even see Darryl.

Manager Darryl: I felt fine.

Kleiny: No you didn't. You had really bad jet lag. You were going to sleep at 7am and staying awake all night.

Manager Darryl: Other than that, I was fine.

Then Dan hit us with a bombshell. I was in Stevenage with Darryl, buying some props for a prank on Kleiny that we were filming, when Dan called. Kleiny was driving to his dad's. Bear in mind, this clothing project hadn't started after LA. It had been going for the best part of two years, so we could be ready to launch when we hit a million followers.

'I need to talk to you,' Dan said over the phone. He told us everything. How the clothing range wasn't going in the right direction and it would be in our best interests if he pulled out.

I'm sorry. What?

Dan repeated himself. He made it official. Some of his previous calculations hadn't been correct. When he redid them, the numbers didn't add up. Continuing wasn't an option.

We were back to square one.

The three of us were on the line in disbelief. We'd just lost all our investment, the best part of £50,000. I started laughing. I was so shocked I started laughing. So did Darryl and Kleiny.

It wasn't our best option for Agent Dan to pull out. But it was Agent Dan's best option.

Dan finished his side of the call and the three of us stayed on the line.

'Boys,' I asked. 'Are we done?'

Kleiny: We were.

Manager Darryl: We were.

Woody: The next day we called a team meeting. Over the years, we've learnt what to do when we get a setback. The direction from our meeting was clear.

Where are we going from here?

How are we getting there?

What are the positives of what has happened?

The positive was obvious. We now had full control. It was agreed that I'd call Bianca and put LUC back in motion.

'You alright, B? What's going on?'

'Yeah, I'm not bad. How about you?'

'I just need to talk to you about LUC. We've split with Dan and need to get an action plan in place ASAP.'

'Great. No problem. When are we going to start?'

Right away. That's the positivity we want to surround ourselves with.

Kleiny: It's a lesson. Everything we've encountered throughout our struggle has been a lesson. We go through it, learn from it, then come out the other side stronger. It was time to get the ball rolling again.

Manager Darryl: No business has gone perfectly. If you make a mistake then hold your hands up.

Woody: People make mistakes in business. One mistake with the clothing project doesn't change the fact that Dan's a great person and a great businessman, just not necessarily for us at that stage of our journey.

We cancelled our exclusive contract with him. We weren't shutting the door on him. We were just opening it to others.

It was time to dream big.

CHAPTER 22
SIX FIGURES

CHAPTER 22

SIX FIGURES

Kleiny: In the three months after our second LA trip we quadrupled our following from 250,000 to 1,000,000. The three months after our third trip to LA were disappointing in comparison...NOT! We managed to treble our following, from 1.7 million to 4.7 million. That's right. We grew by a million followers each month.

Woody: When you get growth like that, it becomes a case of 'how far can we take this now?' Ten million by Christmas? Okay, let's go for it.

Kleiny: The thing with social media is that the quicker you get there, the harder you can fall. It's easy to be forgotten, even when you're followed by millions. That's why you can never rest. The best can always get better. Success means that it's even more important to be regular with your content, keep getting your message out there, keep manifesting future successes.

Woody: Being a proper creator is delivering every day you possibly can. It's not just about having an online presence. To deliver every day, you have to put in an incredible number of hours and sacrifice so much. Eventually you'll start seeing results.

Kleiny: One of our creator mates from LA told us about Facebook Monetization. It had just kicked in over in America and our mate had made $11,000 from one video on Facebook. Wow! We couldn't believe it.

One month later, Facebook Monetization arrived in the UK. We hadn't really been posting to Facebook much because the platform had slashed creators' reach. It was hard to get your video seen. Instead, we'd been focusing on Instagram. That meant we had plenty of content that had never seen the light of day on Facebook.

To qualify for Monetization you needed to have a certain number of followers and have 30,000 minutes' worth of watch time on videos that were at least three minutes long.

Inspired, we put together a few compilation videos, made sure they were three minutes long, then uploaded them to our Facebook page, not really knowing what to expect.

In November 2018 we received our first-ever payment from Facebook. That was a relief because we'd been unsure whether we'd be able to rack up 30,000 minutes of watch time in the first place. Then we saw the figure and didn't know how to react. I'd never seen so many zeros in my life.

Woody: We received a life-changing, six-figure sum from Facebook, just for doing something that we'd been doing for free for the previous six years. It was surreal. There were no brand deals involved. Just pure views.

Manager Darryl: That sorted out the investment for our clothing range. It helped even out the £50,000 we reckoned we'd spent over the years on props, costumes, editing, equipment and travel.

Kleiny: You can take it back as far as the Leicester Square days. Six years later, we had been rewarded for our graft.

Woody: Gamble big to win big. Until the money from Facebook came through, we were relying on brand deals to keep us ticking over. We'd received a bit of money from YouTube – but literally a few hundred dollars here, a couple of hundred dollars there. We were still all working in our day jobs – six years after launching our pages!

Kleiny: And the best thing is that we're nowhere near where we want to be in our journey yet.

Woody: There are occasions when we have to pinch ourselves. People recognise us in the streets now. It seems weird to me. I've done nothing special. I just make videos. It's surreal.

CHAPTER 23
HOW WE DID IT

CHAPTER 23

HOW WE DID IT 🤔

Woody: The previous chapters lay out the answer to how we rode the wave and grew to millions of followers. Do you still think it was luck?

Kleiny: Even now we have creators approach us, asking us for our hack. Some even spread rumours that we had friends at Instagram who were giving us followers for free. Obviously that wasn't the case. We did have a hack. It was simple, really. Our hack is hard work: filming as much as we could, uploading as much as we could, interacting with our audience as much as we could, all while believing in our dream and doing whatever we could to make it work.

Woody: If you break it down, our journey is like one of the 'Stick It In That Old Thing' videos we do. These videos are essentially trick-shot compilations. They look amazing and give the impression we achieved the trick shot first time. But that's rarely

the case. To go viral, they have to be ridiculously hard to do, which can take time.

Recently we were filming a 'Stick It In That Old Thing' where I was lying on my back and attempting to flick a slipper over my head and onto a door hook.

Four hours after my first attempt, we're still going.

My knee is in bits, every little flick brings even more pain. Darryl's bum hurts because every time I flick the slipper and it misses, he stands up to collect it and put it back on my foot.

We don't know when I'm going to finally land the slipper on the hook. We just know that it's going to happen, so we keep grafting and keep believing.

We've gone too far to give up now. We don't have time to lose. Once you've invested four hours of your time you have to see it through, otherwise it's a waste.

It's past midnight and we're both starving.

Darryl gets the pizzas in. We'll just have to catch up on sleep the next night.

Six hours after my first attempt, I finally land it. We stay cool, calm and collected as if it's normal. Then as soon as the camera switches off we go absolutely crazy and celebrate like mad.

That's not luck. That's hard work. You create your own LUC in this world. When people watch the video, they see me flick the slipper onto the door hook first time and think: 'What a lot of fun he's having.' They don't see the hours of struggle or the pain I was in. But that's what we had to put in to get the result we wanted.

I'll tell you what luck is.

Luck (n.)
- An area you visit. The more you
visit that area, the more chance you
have of making something happen.
(Source: Woody and Kleiny)

Kleiny: 'Stick It In That Old Thing' epitomises our mindset, our struggle, and our journey.

The harder you work, the luckier you get. It's a big part of our philosophy. That's why we drive for four hours to get one photograph for our Instagram page. That's why we film for ten hours to get five minutes' worth of footage for a YouTube vlog. Often, we won't use any of that footage and are back again the next day to film. We're exhausted and frustrated but, as soon as that camera starts rolling, the adrenaline kicks in and we're back at 100mph, full of energy.

There's been so much sacrifice along the way. For the vast majority of our journey, we were earning nothing from social media. Yet it was still a full-time job on top of our day jobs, which were also full-time. Each platform needs a different kind of content. What works on YouTube doesn't necessarily work on Facebook. You've got to tailor content for Facebook, Instagram, Instagram Stories, IGTV and YouTube, as well as our podcasts and so much more.

Woody: All those years of finishing work, heading into London to film, getting back at silly o'clock in the morning and then waking up a few hours later to go back to the day job. That's what was needed.

The weekend was a rest because we didn't have as much coaching work to do and could spend most of the day filming.

What do you think our mates were doing every weekend?

We've had to miss out on so much. I've had to miss out on seeing my son, on spending time with Lucy. It's not easy. It's never easy. But if you want to reach the top then you have to make sacrifices. I accept that, and I wouldn't change a thing.

Kleiny: I was speaking to a girl and she asked what I was doing on Sunday. I told her that I was working. 'It should be illegal to work on a Sunday,' she replied.

It's a different mindset.

Eventually we may be able to enjoy our Sundays. Eventually Darryl may be able to play his Xbox again. But until we reach our end goal we'll continue to sacrifice.

Woody: Hard work and sacrifice are our hack. Having a like-minded team is our cheat code. They enable us to take ourselves to the next level. We're constantly trying to get there. It doesn't matter what anyone else is doing. We always focus on ourselves. We're our own competition because everything that we do, we try and make bigger than what has come before it.

It won't always happen. Even now we get a bit of dirty water. We're still making mistakes. We'll carry on making mistakes, even when we have ten million followers. You can never reach perfection. But you should always strive for it. If you push for champagne, the worst you'll get is fine wine.

Kleiny: And now we have our formula. We've been together as a partnership for more than a decade. We know from that experience what brings success on social media.

Woody: That's why we were able to help 'Calendar Girl' grow towards a million followers. And not only her. @WoodyandKleinyExtra is approaching the million. My six-year-old son, Bailey, has his own Instagram page. He doesn't understand the magnitude of it, but right now he's got the best part of 200,000 followers watching him floss and pull funny faces. He's even being recognised on the street. Manager Darryl isn't employing our strategy but has got tens of thousands of followers.

Manager Darryl: I'm on fire.

Woody: Brandon and Gabs are both using our formula and seeing impressive growth. We're also fortunate enough to be mentoring upcoming creatives and helping them to grow.

Kleiny: We've spoken a lot about drive and determination, and there's no point in trying to follow our formula if you have no drive and determination. Ultimately, though, we couldn't be where we are today without flipping our mindset, embracing positivity and visualising our success. Our setbacks have given us our drive, our adversity has inspired creativity. All the negatives that we've experienced have come together and made us so powerful. Unbreakable.

Woody: That's The Social Struggle. Would we change any of it? Absolutely not.

Kleiny: We've come through The Social Struggle and made it out the other side. Now we're in control of what we're doing, I can't wait to see where we can take it.

Anything is possible.

And we're just getting started.

'ANYTHING
IS POSSIBLE'

FEAR KILLS DREAMS
#WAKPACK

FOLLY
LEE
NAVIGATION
BRIDGE

RIVER LEE NAVIGATION
74

The Vision Board

1 Grow to ten million followers on every one of our major social media platforms
2 Become the world's biggest entertainers
3 Receive a cheque for £5 million
4 Get jobs as TV hosts
5 Buy a mansion
6 Maintain connections with our followers and engage with even more people around the world
7 Make LUC a well-established global brand
8 Remain healthy and happy with our friends and family
9 Inspire a generation to follow their dreams and aspirations. You can be anything you want to be!

ACKNOWLEDGEMENTS

Woody: So now we've come to the part of the book where we thank all those who have helped us get into the position where we are today.

Kleiny: I'd like to thank myself for all this hard work.

I'd like to thank myself for having no days off.

I'd like to thank myself for never quitting.

I'd like to thank myself for being me at all times.

Kleiny, you a bad mother –

Woody: Haven't you just copied and pasted that from Snoop Dogg? 😂

Manager Darryl: Don't listen to him, Kleiny, you stay humble. There are a few people I'd like to thank: my mum, dad, brother, family members and friends who encouraged me to try and live in my own fantasy world rather than settle for reality! To Seth Burkett and Ian Ridley, thank you for giving Woody and Kleiny a chance to share their story. Then there's Will, Jonna, Cornell, Harry, Lucy, Bailey, Brandon, Bianca, Gabs, Dan, Harley and all those others who have helped us achieve our goals in so many different ways.

I would also love to thank anyone that told me 'no', who laughed at me, questioned what I was doing or discouraged me. You were the ones that gave me strength and the fire in my belly to make all of this work!

To anyone who has liked, shared, followed, subscribed supported or even watched anything Woody and Kleiny have done: without you none of this would have been possible.

Finally, I'd love to thank my dog, Saph.

Kleiny: You what?

Manager Darryl: Haha, I'm joking. The final thank you has to be to Woody and Kleiny: the ones who put so much of their faith in me and have also shown me nothing but love. Even if it's tough love, you are the ones who have watched me grow and have been a part of that. This is not a work relationship or a friendship. It's family!

Woody: Writing this book has been one of the most fun, liberating and therapeutic experiences of my whole life. It's been one hell of a struggle on this mad journey, but a journey I wouldn't change in any way. The Social Struggle has made me appreciate all the highs we are now embracing, which are so much more

rewarding after the blood, sweat and tears that we have given to the cause.

I have a few people to thank. First, many of my family and friends – whether you thought I was simply bonkers chasing some mad dream, or truly believed in our vision, I'm pretty sure you were still rooting for us. This includes but is not limited to the following special people...

My mum and dad, who have shown me pure love and support in anything I choose to do. My step-parents, my little brother Michael, my sisters Kate & Amy. My nephews Kane, Dylan, James and Joseph, my two nieces Aoife and Rose. A shout-out to Aden (PLZ) Durde, Adem and @Disneyfind Roisin too. To all my mates – you know who you are – with special mentions to my brothers Nick, Anthony and Bassy. I'm blessed to have you all support me and rip me apart twice as much. There's no doubt that it keeps my feet well and truly grounded.

Then on to our team. We've built an army and this lot are ready to fire on all cylinders. I present to you: Team WAK!

Manager: Darryl Stewart

US consultant: Tim Frasier

Director/cameraman: Brandon Baum (the most talented person I know, alongside Anthony Roberts, lol!)

Director/cameraman: Jonna McIver

Photography/cameraman: William Ferguson

Editor: Gabs Djanogly

Financial manager: Matt Dede

Clothing-line manager: Bianca Sobell

The pension: @baileylennon

A special mention to Agent Daniel Levine, who bought into us at the very start, believed in us and gave many years of hard work. We may have parted ways, but we truly hope your business and dreams continue on the same positive road. To Sunil Singhvi at Instagram, you are a legend and every rep should want to follow in your footsteps. To people like my good friend Frank Thompson, who supported me with his amazing camera skills back when I was sixteen years old, continued to help me at times when I needed it, all the way up till now. Having people like you around, giving to me for nothing in return, simply out of love, has truly helped my growth from the very start; I thank you dearly. Also to Seth and Ian for giving us the opportunity to write this book – it's an honour to have your backing.

Then there's the #WAKpack, our fans/followers. Without you we are just a few pages on social media. We try to get back to all comments, which is now nearly impossible. However, we want you to know that we appreciate every like, every share, every comment and every view that you give us. Without you we are nothing, so thanks for joining our journey and fuelling our dreams. We can't wait to continue pumping content for you guys and seeing where this crazy ride ends up. So if you're on board, strap yourself in and let's go get it!

The manager... Darryl, you're one hell of a special guy and that's why you get two mentions, lol! Thanks for caring as you have from the very start. Thanks for sharing our vision and always throwing yourself into anything needed to get the job done. As I always say, you are the 'AND' in 'Woody and Kleiny' and always will be.

Now on to my wife, Lucy, and my son, Bailey. Everything I do and continue doing is to provide all I can for you two. Lucy, you put up with me coming and going at the most random times, and you put up with me working seven days a week most weeks, allowing our home to be used as a film set most days, but most importantly, you support me and the team in our vision. Bailey, you mean everything to me and you make me more and more proud every day. You make me wanna be a better person than I was the day before, and my heart crumbles every time I look at you. Remember, life's for living, so chase your dreams and make sure you dream big. You can and will be anything you want to be – just focus, have fun and never give up. Our little family is just perfect and I love you both very much.

For anyone who knows me well and has read to this point, you may have noticed someone missing. They were never missing and never forgotten. One of my final lines must go to a person I see as a superhero. In life we all go through our own trials and tribulations. However, what I have experienced with you – whether good, bad or indifferent – we have faced it all together. You have been the most consistent person ever in my life. I have a bond with you that is unparalleled and will never be matched. See when you experience certain things and go through stuff with someone to the extent we have at times, it creates an unbreakable bond.

At my lowest points I would look to you for help and guidance, knowing you would save me if I needed it. During my highest moments you would be just as close to enjoy the ride and make sure I stayed well inside my own lane. You are my best friend, mentor and soldier. Make sure you know, just as you have been for me, that I'm always here and ready to go to war with you. My brother Gareth,

I love you dearly and thank you for being the ultimate rock in my life. None of what I have ever achieved, could have been done without you in my corner!

Lastly, you think I'd write all that and forget to raise a glass to my Klein Doggs. Here's to you and us, mate. I'm proud of – and nothing short of blown away by – all you have done from the very start. You've edited a scary amount of hours over the years, driven much of what we have put in place, and you wow me every time with your mindset. You are brave, honest and have got amazing drive that has helped us grow to where we are today. However, above all that and most importantly, you are one hell of a good person. I spend pretty much every day with you, have learnt so much being around you, and couldn't think of anyone else to be on this crazy journey with. I heard a great saying once that I stand by: 'A good leader can be led but only by those they trust.' I have followed your lead many times up till now and will continue to do so, so walk into the fire if you must and know I'll be right behind you. In short, mate: thanks for simply being you!

Kleiny: I suppose I should probably thank some people other than myself after that then...Wowzer, where do I begin? Writing a book about the story of your life is the most surreal process ever. I still have to pinch myself every time I think about it. So here goes...

First and foremost I'm eternally grateful to one of my best friends and double act partner Woody, who inspires me every day to be a better person. We have been on this journey for seven years now and I wouldn't change anything for the world. It is an absolute honour to be in this with you, brother. Thank you for being you.

Manager Darryl, we owe our deepest gratitude to you my man! Honestly you are one extraordinary human being. Without your guidance and persistent help none of this would have been possible.

I would also like to express my deepest appreciation to our team Darryl, Brandon, Gabs, Jonna, Tim, Will, Lucy, Bailey and Bianca! Thank you, guys, from the bottom of my heart. Thank you for believing in us and striving us on to success. The WAK pack: you absolute bunch of legends! Thank you all so much for the support you give us. You continually inspire us every day to make more content and to be the best we can be. #WAKpack

Thank you to my family and friends who believed in us. You guys rock, love you!

Lastly, I would like to thank the family and friends who didn't believe in us and our vision - you gave me so much motivation to prove you all wrong.

Woody: Yeah, I want to thank the struggle and the doubters. I appreciate everything so much more because of you. And one more thing: here's to the future, because I predict it's gonna be one hell of a ride! #LetsGo 🤜🤜🤜

Woody and Kleiny: Thanks from both of us to everyone for supporting us this far on our journey. And thanks to everyone for supporting us with where we're heading next. But let's save the details for the second book...

Woody: Oh, one final thing before you go. Remember when Kleiny leaked my number to the #WAKpack? Well now it's time for payback...

Please let him know what you thought of this book. He'll only be too happy to take your calls.

07506858635. You know what to do.

THE #WAKPACK SPEAKS

WE PROMISED TO FEATURE THE BEST HUNDRED COMMENTS FROM THE #WAKPACK AFTER ANNOUNCING OUR BOOK ONLINE. SO HERE WE GO...

@zimsunshine2482 Got my mum to watch ur vids. She is 75 yrs old and suffers from anxiety. Watching ur vids has made a difference. Thanks keep it up.

an_artrovert_introvert You are the masters at creating appropriate pranks for everyone to enjoy instead of cruel pranks. Thank you!

kalliyangnem I love your videos they are sooooo funny especially when Bailey is in them

callumgr712 You guys inspired me to create content and now it's my dream to be a YouTuber. Thank you so much for making AMAZING videos.

Michael Hardin Every time there's something bad going on I just click on your page and it's always good for a laugh or two. So keep on keeping on bros. You never really realise just how big of impact that you really make on someone's life.

Omar Babo definitely this book is gonna be full of fun and joy

Paul Seenan boys to men go big or go home you guys have made it with top quality content and ya made millions laugh nothing better than making people happy big up from Belfast

Sarah Garrett Do I want to say no to this book NOT TODAY MATE NOT TODAY! :)

لارا بشر It's the first time I feel so excited to read a book in all the 12 years ago at school

Liz Eyeington Looking forward to reading the book alongside my son, we share a love of your vlogs. The team are all fab! Big shout out to Bailey, what a little star!

Michael Hardin You guys are awesome. My family catches hell over me copying your pranks LMBO.

Ashley Johnson You guys are amazing, funny as hell Bailey is so cute he has the best people to look up to.

LUC

AVAILABLE TO BUY NOW

WWW.LUCCLOTHING.COM